ADVERTISING MASTERY

CREATE ADS THAT SELL

ASHISH GUPTA

Copyright © Ashish Gupta
All Rights Reserved.

This book has been published with all efforts taken to make the material error-free after the consent of the author. However, the author and the publisher do not assume and hereby disclaim any liability to any party for any loss, damage, or disruption caused by errors or omissions, whether such errors or omissions result from negligence, accident, or any other cause.

While every effort has been made to avoid any mistake or omission, this publication is being sold on the condition and understanding that neither the author nor the publishers or printers would be liable in any manner to any person by reason of any mistake or omission in this publication or for any action taken or omitted to be taken or advice rendered or accepted on the basis of this work. For any defect in printing or binding the publishers will be liable only to replace the defective copy by another copy of this work then available.

Contents

1. What Is Advertising 1

SECTION 1: ADVERTISING BASICS

2. Ad Principles 5

3. Process Of Creating Ads 18

4. Elements Of Ads 20

SECTIONS 2 - ADVERTISEMENT REVIEWS

5. Advertisement Reviews 25

SECTION 3 - CREATING GREAT ADS

6. Creating Ads 43

7. Search For Ideas 46

8. Stealing Great Ideas 52

9. Creating Great Ads Consistently 71

10. Some More Helping Points 73

11. The Beginning (conclusion) 79

CHAPTER ONE

WHAT IS ADVERTISING

Before we begin, let us first understand what exactly is advertising. Earlier, we saw how marketing is different from advertising. Both these terms are often used interchangeably and are considered to be the same, but we know this is not true.

Advertising is a paid form of communication with a large audience in order to promote products or brands. The key word here is 'paid form of communication'. Advertisement is only a part of entire marketing system and in no way, the complete campaign. Many marketers have found great success without a single penny being spent on an advertisement.

So, we can conclude by saying that advertising is a small subset of marketing. However, if done well, it can do magic to sales of products. Creating ads, therefore, is one of the most important functions for businesses.

However, on one hand, getting an agency or an expert to create ads might end up being expensive for small businesses, and on the other hand, business owners with no prior training, who try creating ads themselves may not find enough success because they often ignore the basic principles of creating advertisement.

Now that we are here, we will discuss some important concepts that need to be kept in mind while creating ads that work well i.e. ads that sell the products and are remembered by the customers. To give you some clarity, this ebook is divided in three major sections.

First, we will discuss few important principles that are a pre- requisite for creating ads. Second, we will see a few ads and review each of them. Lastly, we will see how great advertisers create ads so that you can start creating them for your business. Let us get started.

SECTION 1: ADVERTISING BASICS

CHAPTER TWO

AD PRINCIPLES

1. DO WHAT YOU MAY, THEY MUST REMEMBER YOU

This is the very first rule of advertisement. Do whatever you want to in your ad, the bottom line is the viewers must remember you. If the viewers do not remember you, the chances of them purchasing from you decreases significantly.

Therefore, whenever creating any ad, always ask yourself, "Will people remember this ad?" If the answer is no, you know you need to keep looking for ideas. To do this you need to create something that is new or different.

If your ad is just like everyone else, what is the probability of viewers remembering your ad? None. So, always remember, whenever creating ads, do something new or different. Every single time.

Ads people do not remember

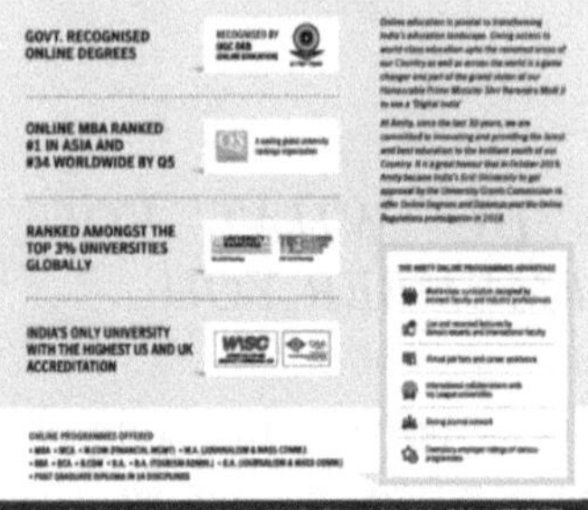

2. *ADVERTISING MUST SELL*

The primary purpose of advertising is to sell a product or service. Basic as it may sound, people often forget this fundamental rule. They confuse selling with creativity. In an attempt to make creative ads, they often forget that an ad has to sell.

No matter how creative an ad is, if it does not sell, it is not a good ad. So, whenever creating advertisements, focus on selling. Creativity should act as a catalyst to this process and should not be the primary focus.

3. *DO NOT JUDGE ADS BASED ON SALES*

Contradictory as it may sound to the previous point, not all ads that sell are good. Even the dullest advertisement can do well at sales, but it does not mean you should get into the habit of creating such ads.

So, remember, all ads that do not sell are bad, but all ads that sell are not necessarily good. Few of them are bad too. Do not judge ads based on sales solely.

4. *LESS IS MORE*

Whenever people feel cluttered with information, they create a wall around themselves and do not let anything go to their brains i.e. they go on an information diet. Since this is a chaotic world where everyone is trying to say something, it makes the customer doubt even the genuine ones.

This is the primary reason why prospects tend to forget most of the advertisements they come across. That is why the lesser you say, the better it is. People have less to remember and because of that, the chances of them remembering your message is very high.

At the same time, those who say a lot in the advertisement, give a lot to remember to the customer and because that will require a lot of effort, the customer tends to forget the message. This is also related to the principle of focus that we had discussed in the previous ebooks.

The lesser you say, better it is. It requires less effort from the viewer's end. Clearly, the viewer has to put in much more effort to read the school ad as compared to the gym ad.

5. DELIVER MESSAGES IMAGINATIVELY AND FREELY

In marketing and advertising, it is not just what you say that matters, equally important is how you say it? If you deliver an old message in a creative manner, the chances of people remembering are higher than a new message delivered in a dull way.

So, whenever advertising, deliver messages that you want to using imagination. Be free with choices and do what you may, to be remembered.

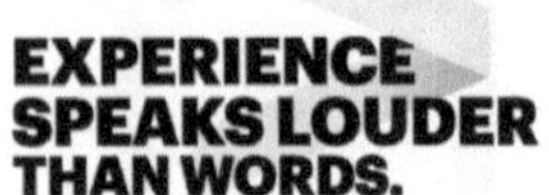

You can see that these ads say things in a boring manner. In a manner that is not very creative and appealing and therefore reduces the chances of them being remembered.

You can see that these ads say things in a very creative and free manner. The chances of them being remembered is very high. So, when creating ads, take complete liberty of freedom.

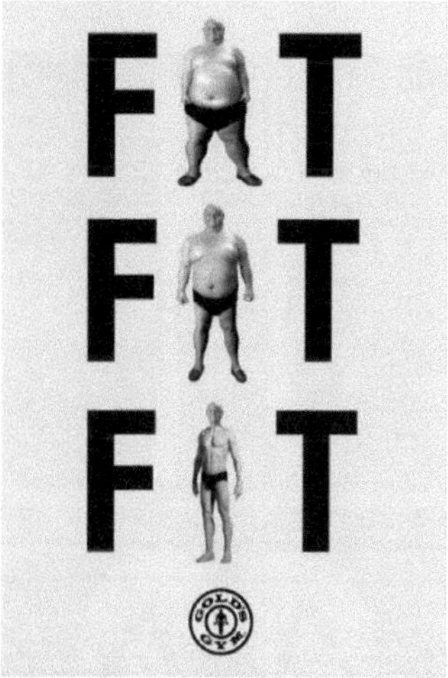

6. CONCEPT BASED ADS

All good advertisements are a part of a marketing concept. None of them operate in a vacuum, they are a part of the bigger picture. When creating ads, focus on concepts rather than simply creating ads for creativity's sake.

All good ad campaigns have a common direction in which they are headed. For example, if L'Oreal celebrates women's power then all the ads over at least six months focus on the same. Make sure that all ads you are running are in one direction.

Only then will you mean something to the customers. On the other hand, if you stand for three different things, you would end up standing for nothing i.e. you would mean nothing to the prospect.

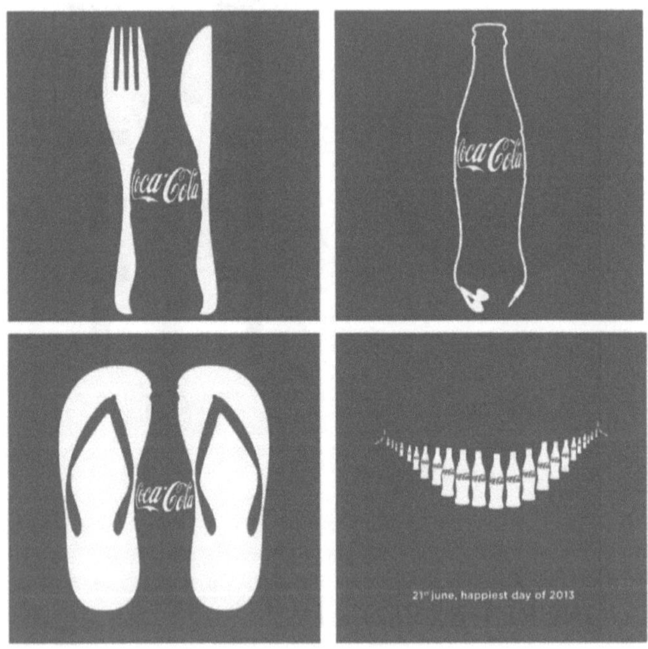

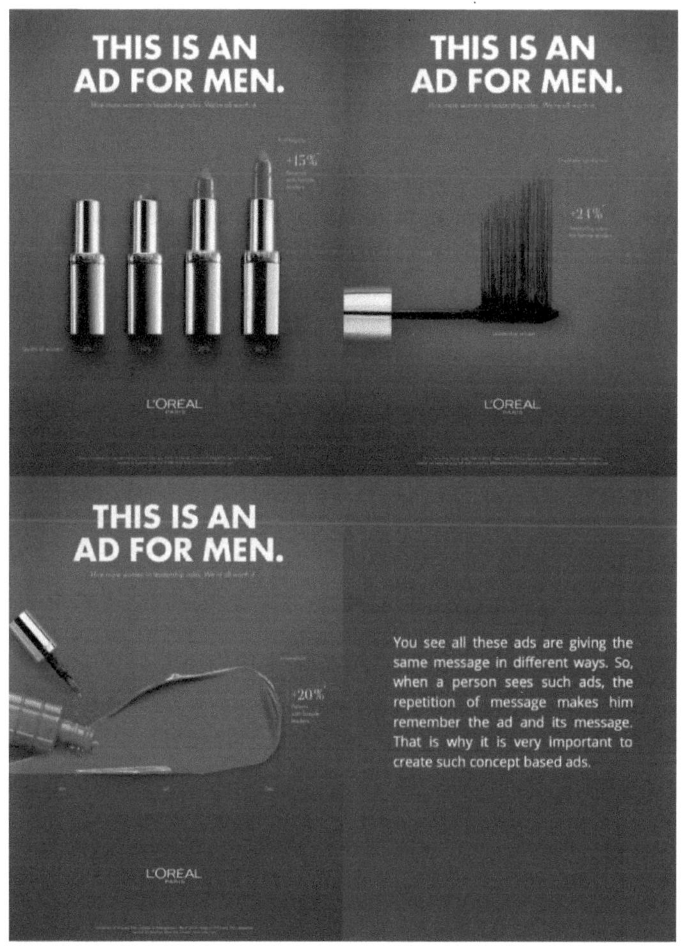

7. ADS SHOULD APPEAL TO EMOTIONS AND NOT INTELLECT

"The brain thinks but the heart decides." This is an age-old saying in the marketing industry that says that the brain processes all the facts but it is ultimately the heart that decides what to buy and what not to buy.

Each decision taken by individuals is influenced by their emotions and psychology. That is why it is best for advertisers to appeal to emotions rather than intellect. They must appeal to psychological gains and pains and social gains and pains that we discussed in the ebook 'Know Your Customer'.

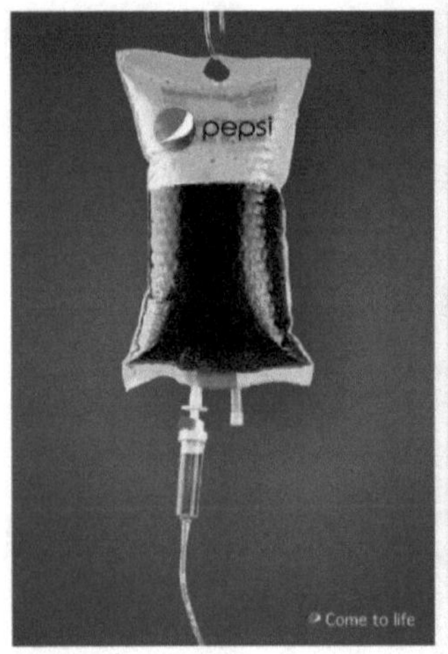

These ads deliver their messages by appealing to emotions. These ads generate better responses in B2C products.

These ads deliver their messages by appealing to the intellect. These ads generate better responses in B2B products.

8. ADVERTISING IS A BATTLE BETWEEN RESEARCH AND CREATIVITY

Advertisements are created by creatives whereas are constrained by research. Even though, the creatives would want their creative minds to wander and look for ideas across, they are constrained by research.

Due to the findings of the research and the decisions regarding what messages are to be sent and what are not to be sent, advertisement becomes a constant battle between research and creativity

9. ADS CAN NOT BE BORING

We already saw that, “Do what you may to be remembered by your viewers.” The first rule to be the one who is remembered by the viewers is plain and basic – Do not be boring. Be new and different. By definition, if you are new and different, you are not boring.

So if you are creating an ad that is just like other ads, or that is similar to ’the way other companies advertise', then your chances of being boring go up manifolds. So, keep in mind, whatever you do, whatever ad you create, you cannot afford to be boring.

Your ads must excite the viewer. Only then there is a chance of being remembered.

10. ADS ARE ABOUT STEALING

“Good Artists copy, great artists steal.” One of our favorite lines about advertising is – “Until you’ve got a better answer, you copy.” This means that most good advertising is copying or stealing. For this, you need to create a large collection of good ads that have worked in the past.

This step takes time but is worth the effort. Once you have collected a pile of ads, you should go through them once every few days. Also, at the same time, you should keep looking for other ads to add to this collection. Every time you go through the ads, few stick in your head.

Next time around, whenever you sit to create ads, you will get ideas already illustrated in this stack. All you have to do is re-do the idea to make it relevant to the context in which you are advertising.

Also, at the time you have a message that is to be drafted into an ad, you can go back to this stack of good ads that you have collected and then refer them back till the time you get an idea. We will talk more about this going forward. But for now, go back to the first line of the ad and re-read that –

"Good artists copy, great artists steal."

PABLO PICCASSO"

Lorose

11. DRAMATIZE THE MESSAGE

The key to great ads is that they take a simple message, at times so simple that it is already well known by the audience and then dramatize the message in such a manner that people end up remembering it. Only the messages that are remembered will make an impact.

If you are claiming a benefit from your product, do not claim it simply, instead portray it in a dramatic manner.

CHAPTER THREE

PROCESS OF CREATING ADS

The process to create great ads begins with research. We learned it all in the ebook 'Know Your Customer' i.e. the different models that can be used to conduct research. Only if you have a strong research base, will you be able to create ads that appeal to your customers.

Without that, it is very difficult for marketers to create good ads that sell. Without adequate research, you might create creative ads but you would not be able to select messages or words that resonate with the audience. So, again we repeat, the first step to creating great ads is to have a good research base in place.

Second, single out a message that is to be delivered. This message will act as a central theme or concept around which all advertising will revolve. Always remember that you need to have a focus on messages in a campaign. You cannot try and say too many things.

Say a few things and say them well. We had discussed a list of questions towards the end of our research ebook 'Know Your Customer'. You can use any single question from this list to focus upon. Stick to one question only.

Once you have done your research and finalized what message you want to focus on – whether on a particular feature of the product, whether, on a particular customer behavior etc., you need to move forward and start creating ads actively.

HOW DOES IT WORK

James Webb Young, a copywriter laid out a five-step process for idea generation. These include the following.

- Gather as much information on the problem as you can. Read, ask questions, meet customers, look at the product, and much more.
- Next, sit down and actively attack the problem after finalizing the message. Look at other ads that you had collected to look for inspiration, basically swimming around in the sea of creativity and new ideas.
- After that, drop the whole thing and go do something else while your subconscious mind works on the problem.
- "Eureka!"
- Lastly, figure how to implement the idea with its details, but your creatives and strategy are taken care of.

This is the exact process of how great ads are created. It is the exact process of how you go forward by allowing your subconscious mind to wander around and look for ideas.

CHAPTER FOUR

ELEMENTS OF ADS

There are few elements of advertisements that apply universally irrespective of the kind of ad being created and the media used for its distribution. These elements remain the same. You can use all of them, a few of them, or add a few elements of your own. Let us have a look at major elements of an ad–

CUSTOMER SEGMENTATION IDENTIFICATION

In our earlier ebooks, we have already seen the importance of customer segmentation in marketing. You need to create ads for different customer segments and together they will form an advertisement campaign. Many ads begin with identifying the customer segment they wish to target.

For example, you would see ads saying – "This ad is for men", "To all the new mothers.." etc. Ads by small businesses must identify a target market and address them. Few large companies do not identify the customer segment as they are well known outside their target market too, but small companies must identify the customer segment in their ads.

MESSAGE

Once the market is identified, the next step is to deliver the marketing message in a creative and dramatized manner. Here, be specific with the message and only deliver one message rather than multiple messages.

Have a focus on the message and try to make it as pictorial as possible. The element that makes or breaks the ad is the message. What is being said and how is it being said determines the success or failure of ads.

OFFER

The next element of the ad is a time-sensitive offer. An offer is a statement of what the person will get in exchange for his time, money, or effort. Large companies often let go of the offer part because they have the budget to keep putting money into advertising without direct selling.

This is not the case with small businesses. If their ads do not get them direct sales, they would have to stop advertising. This is why it is a must that all ads by small companies must have a direct offer. Also, the offer should be time-sensitive which means it should create a sense of urgency.

Only then will the viewer be inspired to take immediate action.

CALL TO ACTION

Once the viewer has seen the message and offer and he has decided to act, the next element should be a clear indication about what to do next i.e. what action to take next, where to go next.

Often marketers miss out on a clear call to action assuming that viewers will figure it out themselves. The truth is that no viewer makes this effort. So, all good ads must have a clear call to action.

TRUST ELEMENT

Lastly, there should be one element in your ad that gets the viewer to trust you. If you are a small business, generating trust is one of the primary roles of marketing.

So, in your ad include elements such as your clientele, your reviews, your ratings, your partners, brand name if recognized, etc. Only if people trust you, will they ever buy from you.

SECTIONS 2 - ADVERTISEMENT REVIEWS

CHAPTER FIVE

ADVERTISEMENT REVIEWS

1 Clearly identifies and addresses the target market i.e. generally it is the men who take decisions regarding tyres.

Man's most precious gift.

A simple and well demonstrated ad. Explains the concept clearly, excellent use of imagery. When delivering a message, using images go a longer way than using texts. Overall, this is a good brand ad.

2

4

Although, this ad can be used for any product, but it will work better for ads directed towards women i.e. they associate more with ring box then men.

Absence of 'Call to Action'. It is a must for all small companies. Also, the ad does not create any form of urgency

3

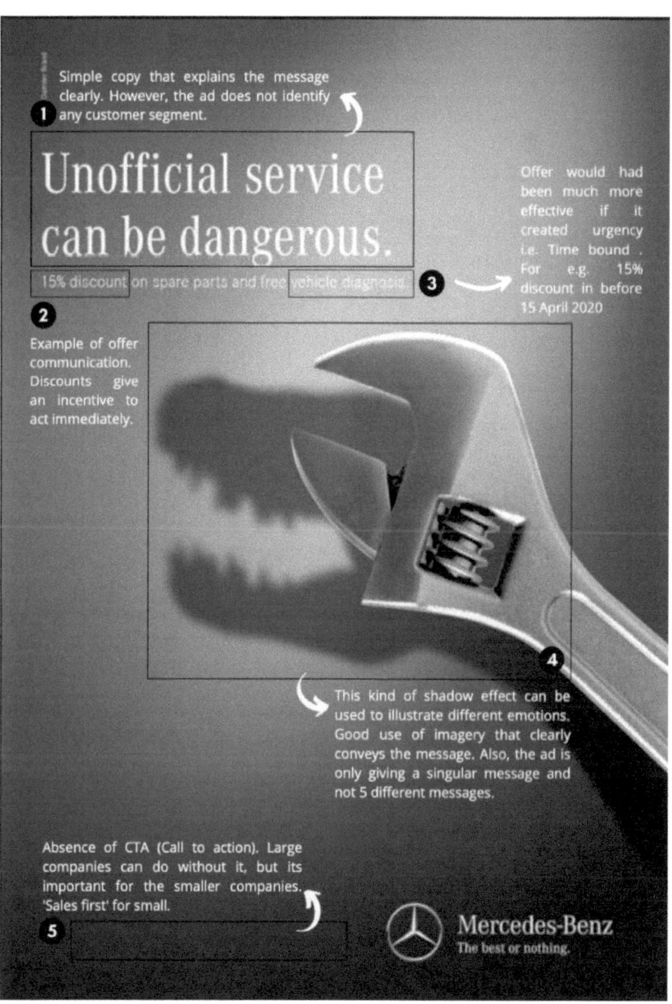

1 Simple copy that explains the message clearly. However, the ad does not identify any customer segment.
Unofficial service can be dangerous.
15% discount on spare parts and free vehicle diagnosis.
2 Example of offer communication. Discounts give an incentive to act immediately.
3 Offer would had been much more effective if it created urgency i.e. Time bound . For e.g. 15% discount in before 15 April 2020
4 This kind of shadow effect can be used to illustrate different emotions. Good use of imagery that clearly conveys the message. Also, the ad is only giving a singular message and not 5 different messages.
5 Absence of CTA (Call to action). Large companies can do without it, but its important for the smaller companies. 'Sales first' for small.
Mercedes-Benz
The best or nothing.

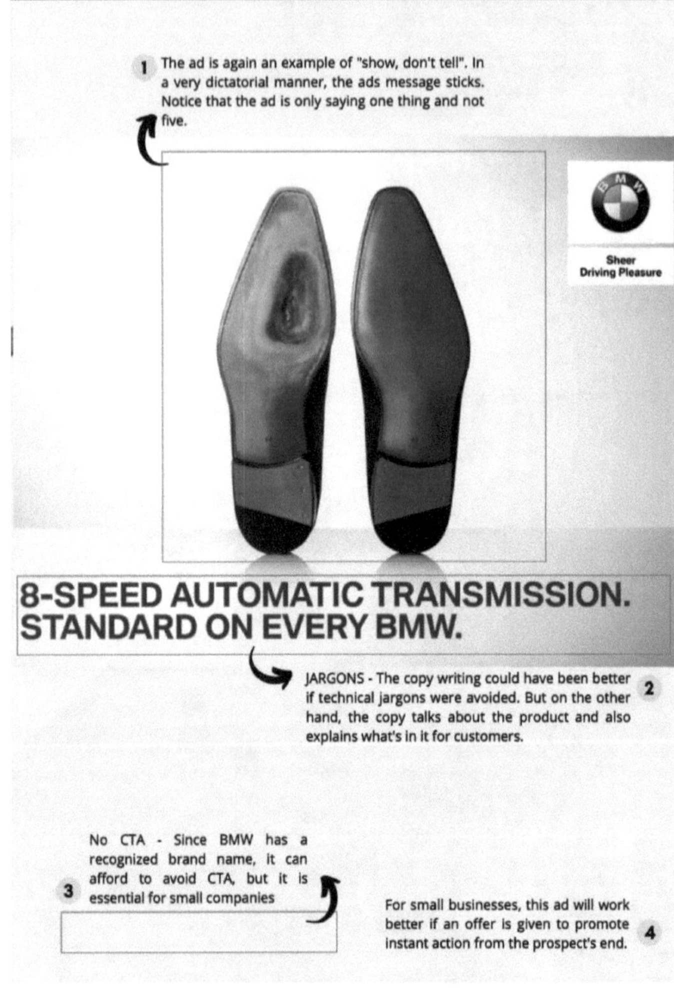
1 The ad is again an example of "show, don't tell". In a very dictatorial manner, the ads message sticks. Notice that the ad is only saying one thing and not five.
Sheer
Driving Pleasure
8-SPEED AUTOMATIC TRANSMISSION.
STANDARD ON EVERY BMW.
JARGONS - The copy writing could have been better if technical jargons were avoided. But on the other hand, the copy talks about the product and also explains what's in it for customers. 2
3 No CTA - Since BMW has a recognized brand name, it can afford to avoid CTA, but it is essential for small companies
For small businesses, this ad will work better if an offer is given to promote instant action from the prospect's end. 4

mondopasta
So good you can't let go.
1
This is a form of 'guerrilla marketing'. It can be done by using unexpected mediums to run an ad. Such ads come as a surprise and are remembered for long.
2
The tagline is written well and explains the ad well.
3
Small business must specify an offer and CTA (call to action)

SAMSUNG
TURN ON TOMORROW
SAMSUNG
MENU
Although, the company displays its product in the ad and the ad has been conceptualized creatively, yet the image could have been composed in a better way.
The ad does not talk about 5 different benefits. It talks about one with focus.
Small business must specify an offer and CTA (call to action)
WB650
15x Super-zoom
webneel.com

Headline addresses the market - We can see that the headline captures the attention of people. It addresses the market segment i.e. those with stomach issues.
1
STOMACH SOUNDING STRANGE?
Image showing the topic - The image creatively delivers the message. You can see that service companies find it difficult to use images.
2
It could be a sign of one of these:
Constipation
Diarrhea
Gas
Intestinal cramps
Abdominal pain
Internal bleeding
If not treated, these can lead to serious chronic ailments later.
Get yourself checked
9663367253
Fortis
3
The ad copy is simple and free of jargons. It is language that viewers would understand. The ad also has its brand name and a CTA mentioned. Overall, this is a good ad that has almost all essential elements.
4
Offer - A time sensitive offer would have caused the reader to take action.

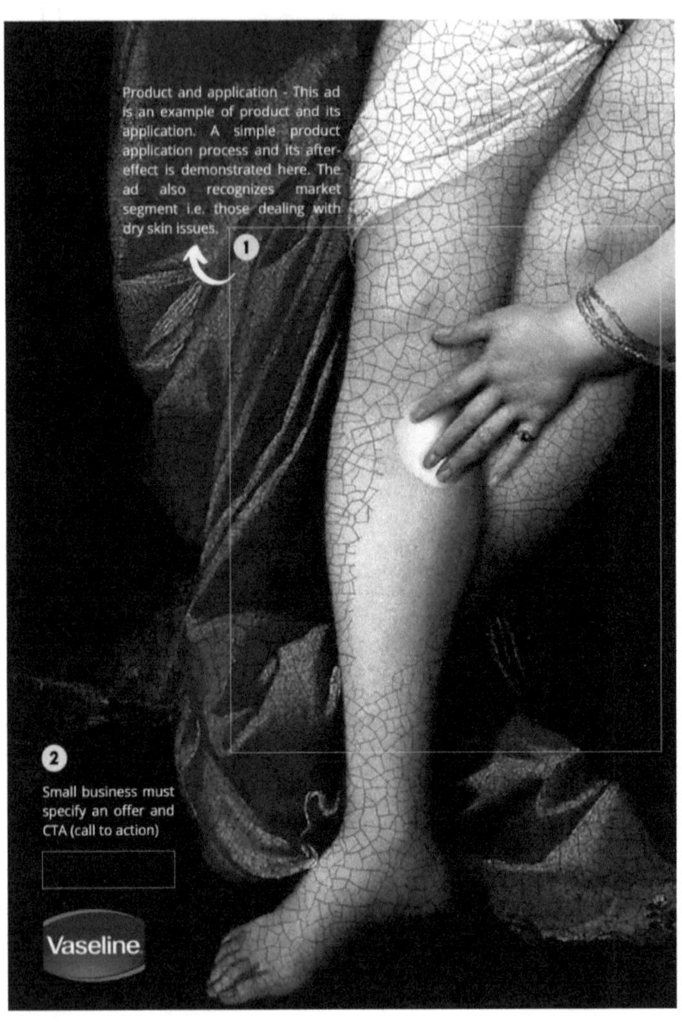
Product and application - This ad is an example of product and its application. A simple product application process and its after-effect is demonstrated here. The ad also recognizes market segment i.e. those dealing with dry skin issues.
1
2
Small business must specify an offer and CTA (call to action)
Vaseline

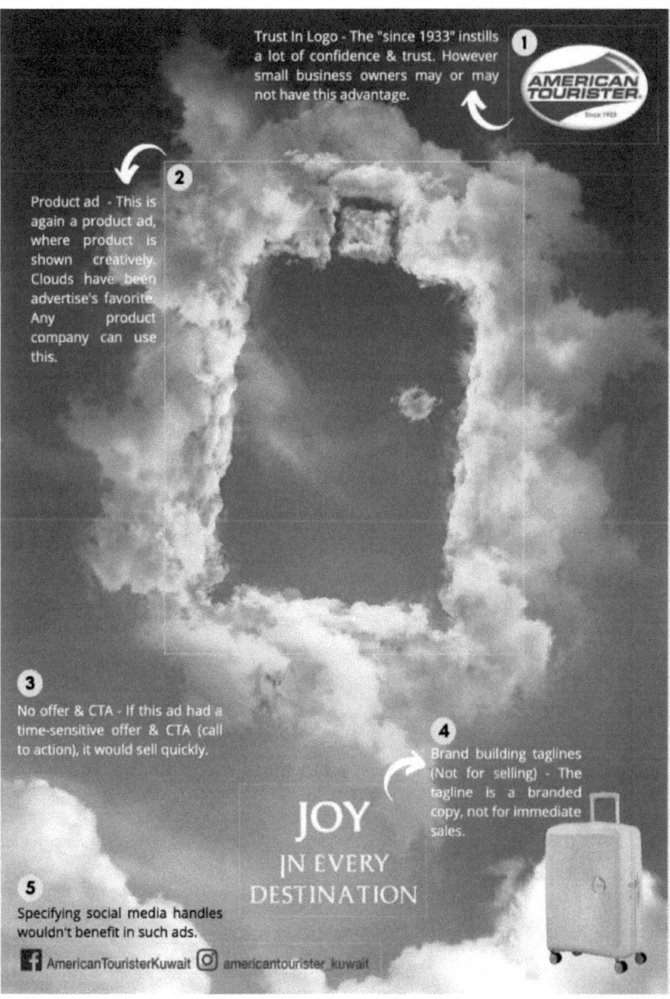
Trust In Logo - The "since 1933" instills a lot of confidence & trust. However small business owners may or may not have this advantage.
1
AMERICAN TOURISTER
2
Product ad - This is again a product ad, where product is shown creatively. Clouds have been advertise's favorite. Any product company can use this.
3
No offer & CTA - If this ad had a time-sensitive offer & CTA (call to action), it would sell quickly.
4
Brand building taglines (Not for selling) - The tagline is a branded copy, not for immediate sales.
JOY
IN EVERY
DESTINATION
5
Specifying social media handles wouldn't benefit in such ads.
AmericanTouristerKuwait
americantourister_kuwait

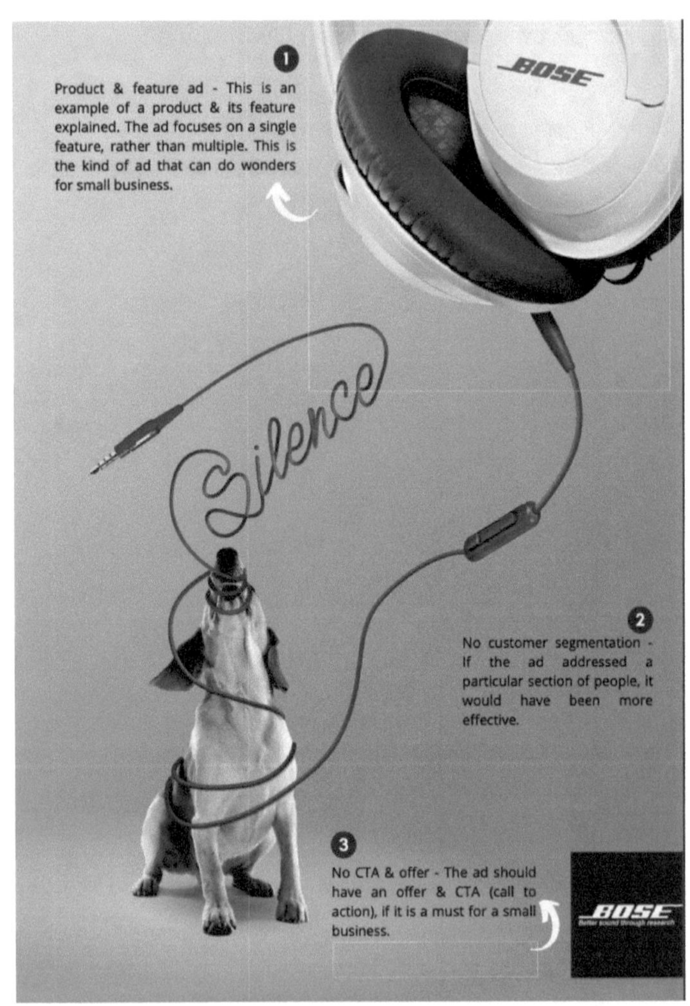
1
Product & feature ad - This is an example of a product & its feature explained. The ad focuses on a single feature, rather than multiple. This is the kind of ad that can do wonders for small business.
BOSE
Silence
2
No customer segmentation - If the ad addressed a particular section of people, it would have been more effective.
3
No CTA & offer - The ad should have an offer & CTA (call to action), if it is a must for a small business.
BOSE

1
Clear Image, gets attention - This ad has a clear image that expresses its message without support of words. The ad gets good attention and is easy for eye to follow.
2
THE SHOW MUSTN'T GO ON
Clear copy - The copy uses an iconic line, that people already know.
3
Clear message, it will be remembered by viewers.
SUPPORT ANIMAL-FREE CIRCUSES
WWW.LAV.IT
4
No CTA - The ad has a clear message, but should have a CTA (call to action) too.

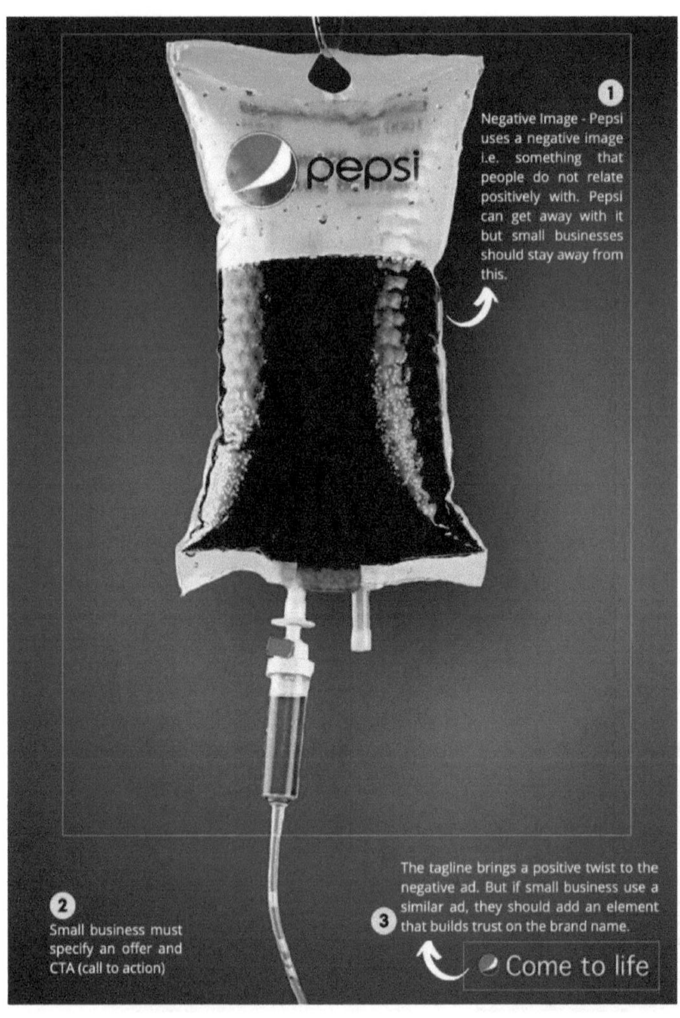
pepsi
1
Negative Image - Pepsi uses a negative image i.e. something that people do not relate positively with. Pepsi can get away with it but small businesses should stay away from this.
2
Small business must specify an offer and CTA (call to action)
3
The tagline brings a positive twist to the negative ad. But if small business use a similar ad, they should add an element that builds trust on the brand name.
Come to life

1 No customer segmentation - Customer segmentation would have made the ad more effective . This ad can be used for any product.
pepsi
2 The ad shows Showmanship of product. They use the concept already known and trusted by the market.
The ad used an Iconic tagline. Such iconic lines are better remembered. 3
GAME OF STRAWS
4 CTA and offer is a must for small business
5 Trusted brand - Pepsi is a renowned brand. But a small business, will need a line to explain what brand is about.

1 No customer identification - The ad does not identify any customer segment. It would have worked better if a customer segment was identified.
The ad copy is short and concise. It can be used by any company that wishes to show 'thrill'. E.g 'Food feels better'. 2
Music feels better.
3 The background image is really thoughtful. It depicts 'goosebumps' i.e. good music quality gives goosebumps to the listener (product consumer)
JBL
Small businesses must have an CTA (call to action) and offer. 4

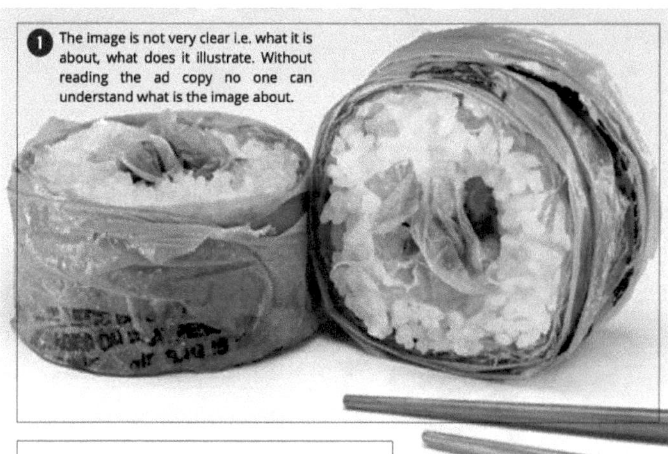

WHAT GOES IN THE OCEAN GOES IN YOU.

2 Clear tagline - The tagline is clear and explains the ad well. can be used by food companies too.

RECENT STUDIES ESTIMATE THAT FISH OFF THE WEST COAST INGEST OVER 12,000 TONS OF PLASTIC A YEAR. FIND OUT HOW YOU CAN HELP TURN THE TIDE ON PLASTIC POLLUTION AT WWW.SURFRIDER.ORG/RAP

3 Too long ad copy. Very few will read. However, it has a clear CTA (Call to Action).

4 Brand explained - It is important for small businesses to explain what their brand is about.

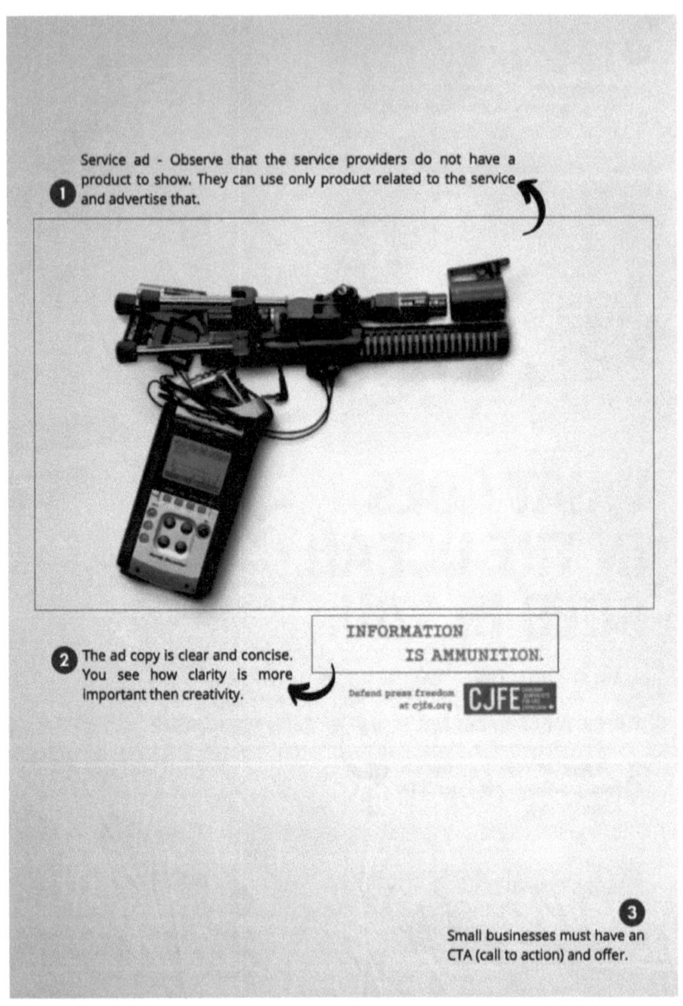

Enter Caption

SECTION 3 - CREATING GREAT ADS

CHAPTER SIX

CREATING ADS

We already saw the broad process to create great ads. We also know the important points to keep in mind while creating ads. Now, let us understand the fine parts of this process. The first step to creating great ads, assuming the research has been done, is to ask a lot of questions.

These questions are asked, not to know more about the product but to get more creative ideas. These can be all absurd questions and ideas. For example, if you are looking at a product to be advertised – Ask a lot of questions as follows:

- What if I invert the product?
- What if I give this product to a toddler? What if I hide in an unexpected place? How is it most useful?
- How is it least useful?
- What day-to-day objects does it relate to? What if I give this product to a monkey?

You can also ask questions about the audience. Questions like:

- What if the consumer never knew about the product?
- What if the consumers stopped using social media?

- What if the customers all went on a vacation together?

Ask all such weird questions and you never know where that one creative idea will come from. We have listed only a few questions. Ask at least 50 such questions. And make sure the questions are not intelligent. Just get as creative as possible.

HUMAN VALUES

The next step is to identify the core human value that you are addressing. No matter how cliché your product is, each product has a role that it plays which is closer to core human values. Now, you need to identify that core human value.

If you have trouble identifying the core human value use this method. All human values and emotions can be categorized into either of the three – greed, fear, and hope. So whatever, you are trying to say in the ad, get closer to the human value of the same.

- For example, Coca-Cola says “Open Happiness”. Whenever you create an ad for Cocacola, you focus is on human emotion ‘happiness’
- When drafting an ad for an insurance company, the human emotion is “Fear”
- When drafting an ad for an adventure sports company, focus on the human value of ‘Adventure’.

Another way to identify the core human values is through Seth Godin’s list. He says all marketing words can be identified into six human values - Anger, disgust, fear, happiness, sadness and surprise. Nothing more, nothing less.

It is up to you to decide which method are you more comfortable with. Identify the human value that you want to focus on and then make sure that each element of the ad is focused on that single human value.

SUBSTANCE VS STYLE

The next step to creating an ad is to focus on the substance rather than the style. Focus on what the ad will contain, the idea, the theme, the message, the offer, the call to action, etc. Focus on all these first before moving on to the details such as fonts, design, etc.

Remember, styles can be changed, fonts can be changed, typefaces can be changed but it's the substance in the ad that gets the ad the required response. So first focus on what to say rather than how to say it.

When thinking about the substance of the ad, consider each of the elements that we discussed earlier. Note down the elements that you want to include and the elements that you want to exclude. Next, think like a lawyer.

Any claim that you make, prove it as a lawyer would. You can create a great ad by making a singular claim and then backing it up with facts so that they earn you creditability. This was was the next step, to focus on the substance of the ad. Next, let's move on to some tricks and techniques that will help you think of creative ideas for your ads.

CHAPTER SEVEN

SEARCH FOR IDEAS

SEARCH FOR IDEAS
LOOK IN THE ENVIRONMENT

Look into the related environment of the product, consumer, or the environment in which the product is to be consumed. You would find amazing ideas themselves. This is one source of ad ideas – look around! Look at the environment of the product, consumer, or the place of purchase.

ASK QUESTIONS

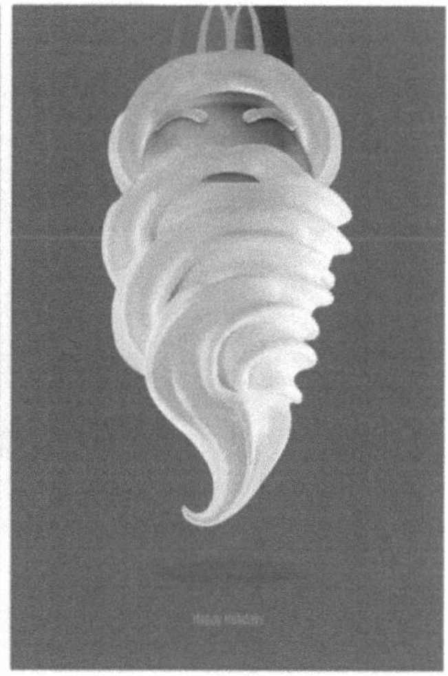

The next trick to look for ideas is to ask a lot of “What if” questions. What If the coke bottle gets legs? What if the coke bottle can start flying? What if my Ice-cream can never melt? What if there is ice cream as big as my car? Ask all such questions which are weird to the human mind but then are the best way to get out of box ideas. More weird the question, better would be ad ideas.

LOOK INTO BASIC HUMAN NATURE

Look for ads that can pictorially represent the human emotion you are trying to communicate. If you want to represent happiness, what are things people associate with happiness? Use those. For sadness use a crying clown or a child with a tear and so on. So, a major source of ideas is to use elements that represent emotion. Such ads stick to the human mind if implemented well.

ASK NEGATIVE QUESTIONS

One of the great ad ideas is to ask negative questions. Ask the reverse of what is established and common to people. For example, here the zebra is chasing the lion whereas it's the other way round. The next ad says "Money can buy time" which is again a negative of "Money can't buy time". Other ideas may include – A tortoise running, a mouse chasing a cat, etc. So, whenever looking for ideas, ask negative questions.

PRODUCT'S IMAGE

A little
TASTE OF
SUMMER

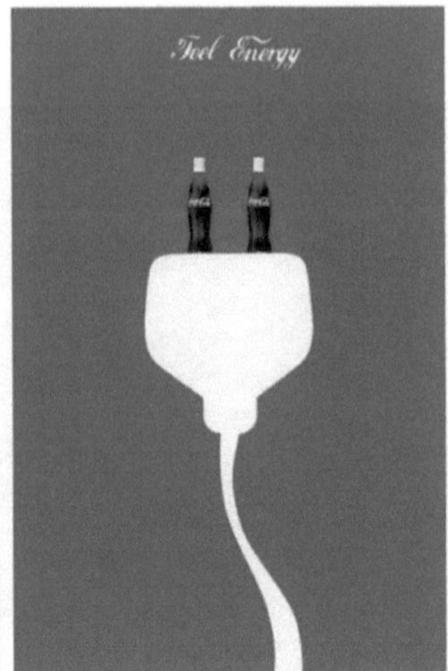
Feel Energy

THE
Signature
COLLECTION

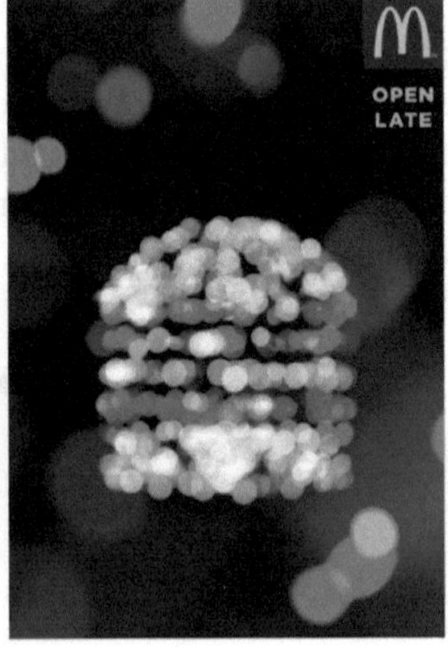
OPEN
LATE

The best of ads take their product and try something creative with it to convey a message. Just sit with the product long enough and you shall have great ideas. However. This is only for product companies. For service companies, they must select an object related to their service and try to do the same with it.

CHAPTER EIGHT

STEALING GREAT IDEAS

So, up until now, we saw a few methods how to get ad ideas. Know that getting the ad idea takes time. You cannot rush through it. Once the idea is there, the execution is pretty much in your control. However, getting the ad idea is not something within your control.

It takes time, practice, and patience. Keep practicing the above-mentioned tricks and techniques. Now, we will discuss another method to get ad ideas. This method is used by even the most established ad creators. The thing is, 'it works'.

The variety of ideas you can get this way is unimaginable. The method we are talking about now is, 'Stealing'. Stealing great ideas from other ads that have worked in the past.

So, we already discussed that all great advertisers have a stack of good ads that they keep collecting over time. You too need to keep collecting good ads over time so that you can refer to them whenever you need an ad idea.

If you are new to this, you can use a shortcut by referring to creative ads on 'pinterest'. But do it initially, only until you are a beginner. After that, try creating your own collection of good ads that you would be using as an inspiration to do your work.

Many good marketers have a stack of ad printouts as high as 3 feet. Once you have this stack ready and you have researched to finalize the message to be communicated, you go through this stack thinking on each ad,

"How can this ad be used for my product and message?" 9 out of 10 times you will not be able to come up with any usage of that ad concept for your product and idea. But 1 in 10 times you will have an idea. If you do this over a large number of ads, you will have a list of ideas for your advertisement.

> *When in the business of advertisement, it is important to have good process for inspiration so that you can continuously keep coming up with good ideas.*

Just keep turning pages in that stack, and good ideas will slowly start coming by. Bizarre things happen when you use this method. For example, you can use the concept of an ad that you saw for an educational institute, for inspiration to create your ad for a child care center.

The products might be completely different but if the concept can be used, you can copy the ad. We will see few examples of how you can use one ad to create another. This is the number one manner in which great ads are created. That is by, stealing. By stealing from other person's ideas.

Many ad creators make it about their ego that all the ideas have to be their own. Well, this is not how creativity works. Creativity needs inspiration.

It can get inspiration from anything anywhere. So, when in the business of advertisement, which is the business of rejection, it is important to have a good process for inspiration so that you can continuously keep coming up with good ideas. If you seek to come up with all ideas on your own, all your ads would have similar concepts and you may lack consistency.

Now, if you are a small business owner or digital marketer and not a full-time ad creator, resorting to such a method is your best bet. The reason is time restrictions. So, start making a collection of all the good ads that you see. Also, do not take advertisements for granted. It can make or break your ideas.

Now let's see how you can steal great ideas. This is an ad by McDonald's showing the showmanship of its burger. Let us see where else can it be used.

Idea 1 – Cocacola could use the same ad and same concept. Just that instead of a burger, it will show the Coca-Cola bottle.

Idea 2 – A laptop company could use this to show the laptop in a similar manner.

Idea 3 – A light company like Philips could use this to show their lights.

Innumerable ideas can be derived from this. You have to think through each ad whether the given ad can be used for the purpose in hand or not. You can also combine multiple ads together to create a new piece of art.

Let's see what all ads can be created using this particular ad as inspiration –

Idea 1 – Companies like Gillette can use this saying –" This Ad is for Women", address a stereotype faced by men, and then illustrate Gillette razors in a similar concept.

Idea 2 – Companies who want to target any particular target market can use this concept. They can either use the product sold by the company or any other object related to the consumer.

Idea 3 – Cigarette companies can also use similar ads.

So you see how any given ad can be used in multiple scenarios. The challenge is for you to identify which ads are suitable for your product in hand and which are not.

This again can be used by multiple product companies. The tire relates to the seller and the ring box relates to the buyer. The ring box also depicts the 'desire' of the buyer.

Idea 1 – A mobile phone can be displayed in the ring box.

Idea 2 – A travel company can use this showing the box and then a famous location from the destination. For example Taj Mahal in the box.

Idea 3 - A bookseller can somehow combine book and specs in an ad. The book relates to the seller and the spectacles relate to the buyer.

This is again a product ad. The method used here is - identify elements related to the message you are giving and use them to demonstrate your product. Let's look at some places where it can be used.

Idea 1- Cocacola wants to say – “Spread Happiness”. Element is related to the message – smile curve. Cocacola can thus use the smile curve to create its bottle and say – Open Happiness

Idea 2 – A mobile company wants to say – Best Music. So, they can use an earphone or speaker signs to create a mobile phone.

Idea 3 – A medical company can show a hospital bed using a medicine capsule.

You now see that such a large number of ad ideas can be generated from each ad. The elements can be copied, or the concept can be copied.

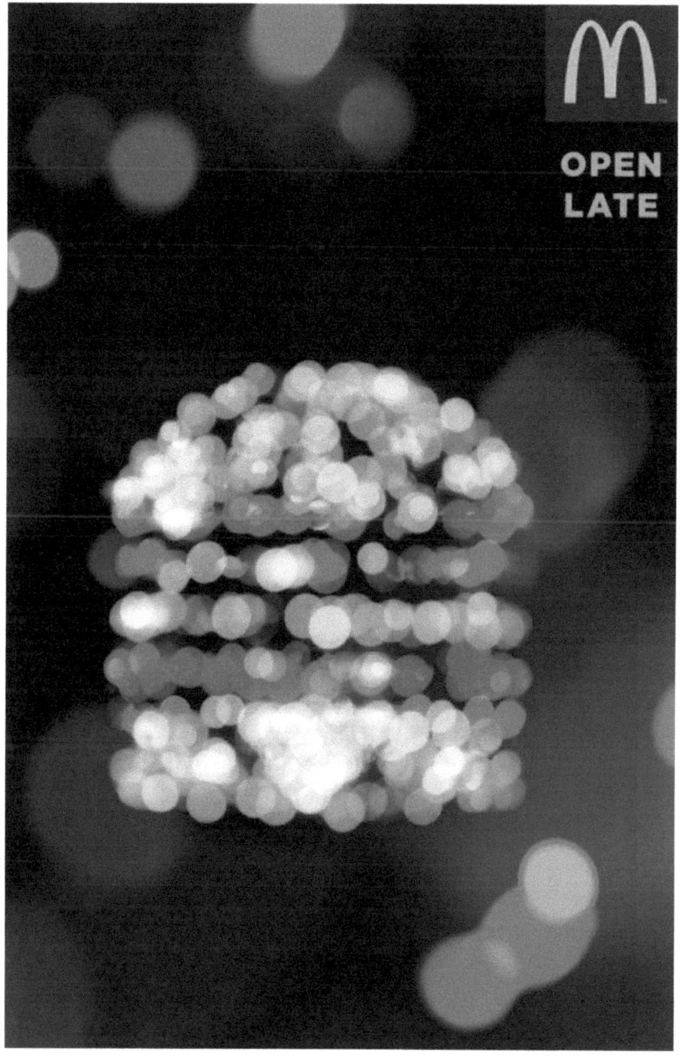

This is one of the most amazingly done ads. This can be used as an inspiration for a large array of ads.

Idea 1 – McDonald's can show this to form a reflection of their burger.

Idea 2 – Nike or Adidas could use it from the reflection of their shoes.

Idea 3 – Any product company can use this to form a shadow of their product. They can also alter the medium on which reflection is achieved i.e. glass, buildings, etc. But, they can be used for an ad.

Idea 4 – Even service companies can use this ad to illustrate any physical object that is related to their service or the customer.

Clouds are one of the most favorite mediums for advertisers. They use clouds to display different products or elements related to the consumer.

Idea 1 – American Tourister in the past has used the clouds to form a luggage shape using them.

Idea 2- Airline companies can use clouds to show airplanes and then deliver the message.

Idea 3- Spectacle companies like Lenskart.com can show the product using clouds very creatively.

In a similar manner, many companies can use this concept creatively to demonstrate their product.

One method to create great ads is to list down all the elements and products related to the consumer and the company. Then these elements can be used to creatively demonstrate the ads. Many ideas can be identified in this manner.

Idea 1 – For an ice cream company, elements related to product or audience – cone, refrigerator, kids, toys, ice cream man, summer, etc. Any of these elements can be used to create an ad.

Idea 2 – For a cricket academy – ball, bat, wickets, ground, floodlights, 11 players, umpires, etc. Any of these elements can be used to create an ad.

Idea 3 – For a bookstore – books, library, spectacles, teacher, Amazon, etc. Any of these can be used to show an ad creatively. A combination can also be used.

Whenever you want to show energy, this ad can be created. This way you can also have specific ads for each theme. Let's see some places where it can be portrayed.

Idea 1 – RedBull or Monster can show such an ad. A charger connected to the drink to depict its "Energy Drink"

Idea 2 – Coffee companies can show exactly the same image.

This ad is again an implementation of using a product related to the message to be given. In this way, each ad can be used as an inspiration for numerous ads.

CHAPTER NINE

CREATING GREAT ADS CONSISTENTLY

This is the way how greatest of ads are created. Maintain a library of good ads that you have collected over time i.e ads that have worked in the past. Then the next thing you will have is an agenda or a product that needs to be advertised.

Next, you need to look for ideas. This is where you refer back to your collection of ads. You go through them one be one. As you go through them, you ask each ad the question – "how can this be used to suit my product?" As you keep doing that, ideas will start to come by. You start listing down ideas. Some ideas will be such that they use few elements from one ad and a few from another. This way you will have listed down a number of creative ideas.

Then it becomes a rejection game so that you can narrow it down to one or two ideas. Then you discuss with your team which idea will work out better.

Follow this to create great ads. Henceforth, you will never face a problem of ads unable to generate the required interest. The success of your ads depends on the library of ads that you have. If you have exceptional work as your reference, your ads would also be good.

If you use mediocre work as a reference, ads will also be mediocre. So be very selective about what ads you add to your library. You can take it on from there. Creating ads that work is as much about the process as it is about creativity.

CHAPTER TEN

SOME MORE HELPING POINTS

GREAT ADS COMBINE DENSITY OF CONTENT WITH THE ELEGANCE OF FORM

So, whenever you are creating ads make sure that you say just enough that is required. Many advertisers make this mistake by adding too much data. Often, a high density of information kills the focus of the ad. Therefore, whenever creating ads, make sure it is not too dense.

The form of the ad should also be good. It should have focus i.e. the eyes should always know where to start from and where to go next.

DO SOMETHING PHYSICALLY BUSY AND MENTALLY EASY

If you are trying to create an ad and are unable to come up with ideas, an exercise used by advertisers is – Do something physically busy and mentally easy. Do something that occupies your physical effort but keeps your mental energy free.

For example, go for a walk, go for cycling, do something in the kitchen that does not require mental energy. All this will allow your subconscious mind to think and come up with creative ideas.

HYPE DOESNT WORK

In advertisements, hype does not work. Hype often leads to over-promising and under-delivering. Therefore, when creating ads, do not try to create hype. Say things that are true. There is a popular saying- “You can trick all of the people some of the time, some of the people all of the time but not all of the people all of the time.” So say things that are true.

If any customer discovers false claims made by your ads, they will never trust you again. And know that, people do not buy from those whom they do not trust. The bottom line is you must never create hype through your ads.

BE VISUAL AND GO SHORT ON COPY

Whenever you are trying to say something, try to say it visually rather than writing it down. It takes effort from people to read something. They are not willing to put in that effort for an ad if it does not get them interested from the word go.

So, to reduce this, focus on creating ads that are more visual in nature. Ads that deliver the message through visual design. It takes less effort from people and thus makes sure that the message is delivered to more people.

Also, then go short on copy i.e. words written. If the message has been delivered through an image, do not re-write the same thing in the text.

USE WHAT IS ALREADY ESTABLISHED

When creating ads, you do not want to re-invent the wheel. Start with what is already established in the mind of consumers and use those metaphors to gain your trust. For example, it is established in the mind of the customer that a shark stands for someone shrewd and opportunistic.

So, whenever you want to establish these facts, use an image of a shark. Use tortoise to show slow and steady. Use what is already established within the mind of the consumer to deliver the message.

AVOID OVERUSED IMAGES OF THE INDUSTRY

Each industry has certain images that are very commonly used. Stay away from the usage of such boring and dull images. For example, for all insurance sellers, a happy family image is used. We know that this could have been a good selling point, but if everyone is using it, it reduces our chance to stand out.

That is why it is important to come up with new concepts. Come up with new images that are not cliché in the industry. Do not be dull and mainstream under any circumstance.

GIVE READERS SOMETHING TO GUESS

Best ads are those that arouse engagement from the viewer. Ads that make the viewer want to do something. Show it to more people. One of the ways to create such ads is those that give readers to guess something. Ads that create curiosity and do not answer leave the viewer with 'tension' and the only way left for him is to 'move forward.

So, keep in mind, ads that cause the viewer to guess something are amongst the best ads as they leave the viewer with tension and inspire action.

CREATE ADS THAT DO NOT LOOK AND FEEL LIKE AN AD

Everyone is exposed to numerous ads around themselves, so much that now people naturally avoid ads. Whenever they see an ad, their natural action is to move over it. They are generally blind towards the ad unless they find something engaging in the first look. So when creating ads, try creating an ad that does not look and feel like an ad.

For that, you should either make it entertaining or educative. If your ads are entertaining, the viewer sees value in the ad itself and generally shares it with more people instead of avoiding it. If your ads are educative, they inspire people to find value in it and therefore they won't be avoided.

However, having said that, it does not mean that you stop selling in an ad. The primary purpose of an ad remains the same i.e. selling.

SIMPLICITY IS EVERYTHING

When creating ads, the simpler it is, the easier it is for the person to understand. If you create an ad that is too complicated, the chances of the viewer understanding your message are very low. The reason for this is the fact that the viewer is not going to put any additional effort to understand the ad.

So, the simpler the ad i.e. the message, the graphics, the metaphors, the elements, the easier it is for the viewer to understand.

SOMETHING SHOULD DOMINATE THE AD

Recall the principle of 'Focus'. All your ads should have a focus i.e. where to begin, where to go next, and then next, and so on. So whenever creating ads something should clearly dominate it – either the headline, image, or body of the ad.

The element that dominates the ad is where the eyes go in the beginning. If there are two elements that are fighting for the dominance, then the trouble begins as the eyes of the viewer will not know where to start from. It creates confusion for the viewer.

The eyes should always know where to start from and for that something should clearly dominate the ad.

BE SPECIFIC AND PAY ATTENTION TO DETAIL

Whenever creating ads, be specific with what you are saying. For example – Do not say, "Product saves you a lot of time". Instead say, "It saves you 4 days." Be specific. Only if you are specific will you be in a position to deliver the message correctly. Say exactly what you want to say and do not beat around the bush.

GREAT COPYWRITING

The next skill required to complete the ad that you have created is to decide on the words that should be written in the ad to complement the visuals. This is called copywriting. If you want to say – The product is available at 10% off.

You can say using multiple words – “Flat 10% of for first 100 users” or “Save 10%” or “Budget tight? Save right. 10% off now” So you see the same information can be given in so many different forms. Copywriting is a completely different skill set that takes time to master.

CHAPTER ELEVEN

THE BEGINNING (CONCLUSION)

With this we end our discussion on ad making. By now, you know all that is required to create visual ads. Now, if you are a small business owner or digital marketer, you know enough to create ads that sell. You need to keep in mind of the basics discussed above.

Keep in mind the elements of good ads, how to get good ideas and lastly, how to create a piece of advertisement that sell.

If you follow all the discussed rules, you may or may not win an award for creativity but you will surely create ads that sell. You will surely create ads that generate attention, interest, desire and action. More importantly, you will be remembered.

So, now you know all that is required to create great ads, rest will come with practice. Start practicing and creating great ads for yourself. Also, do send us all the ads that you create. Also, know that no matter how gifted you are, you will at times make crap. Do not get disheartened. This is the nature of advertising industry. So, let's begin.

Printed by Libri Plureos GmbH in Hamburg,
Germany